Friends at Sea

written by Michael Burgan
illustrated by Sarah Jane Martin

D1413651

**McGraw-Hill
School Division**

New York   Farmington

Imagine that you are sailing through the choppy ocean waters on a bright day. You see a flash of movement over the bow of the boat. Then you see another. You lean on the railing and spot a beautiful creature darting gracefully through the water by the side of the boat. It swims alongside the prow, moving as swiftly as the boat itself—nearly twenty miles per hour. Its body is sleek and blue-gray. This playful creature is a bottlenose dolphin.

Dolphins are found throughout the world. Some species, such as the river dolphins of South America and Asia, are found only in certain areas. These species are found in large rivers such as the Amazon of Brazil and the Ganges of India. The bottlenose dolphin is the most familiar to scientists. This dolphin is found in the North Atlantic and off the east coast of the United States. It is also found in the Mediterranean Sea. One species, known as the common dolphin, can be found in every ocean on Earth.

Dolphins have long fascinated people. The myths of many countries include stories about the dolphin. The ancient Greeks called the dolphin the "sacred fish." We know today that the dolphin is not a fish. It is a mammal and, like humans, must come to the surface of the water to breathe. According to Greek mythology, a dolphin helped the ocean god Poseidon find a mermaid named Amphitrite and bring her to his palace at the bottom of the sea. Amphitrite then became Poseidon's queen.

In another Greek legend, Arion, a poet and musician from Corinth, won a gold prize for his singing in Sicily. As his boat was sailing back to Corinth, the greedy crew turned against him. They began plotting to murder him and take his gold. As a last request, Arion told them he would like to sing one last song. With it, he summoned a school of dolphins. Then, throwing himself off the boat, Arion is carried back to Corinth on the back of a dolphin.

In both of these legends, the gods were very pleased with the dolphin and placed him in the stars. That is why we still refer to one constellation as Delphinus, the animal's Greek name. This idea probably came to the Greeks from India, where this group of stars was also seen as a dolphin.

These stories have come to us from mythology. However, rescue stories have come to us throughout the years from people who have claimed to have survived near-drownings because of dolphins.

Many marine scientists doubted these stories. They asked how a dolphin could know when it was necessary to come to the aid of a person. Since these creatures spent their whole lives in the water and had very little human contact, how would they know whether a human being in the water was helpless and in serious danger?

These scientists had no proof to explain why a dolphin would act as a lifesaver. Yet there are many documented cases in which wild dolphins have come to the aid of people in trouble at sea.

One incident that took place in Florida had an eyewitness observer. A woman was wading in shallow water when suddenly a strong undertow—a dangerous current that pulls away from the shore—began to carry her out into deep water.

The woman was knocked over by the force of the undertow. She inhaled sea water and began to lose consciousness. Just then she felt herself being gently pushed toward the safety of the beach. Half-conscious, she had the impression that someone must be rescuing her.

A man, who had finished doing his morning errands and thought he would spend some time on the beach, saw what had happened. He ran down to the water's edge to help the woman out of the water and was relieved to discover that she was okay. When the woman had revived enough, the man told her that it had been a dolphin, not a person, that had pushed her to shore. The man also let her know that this was the second time he had seen a dolphin rescue a person.

Even if a dolphin understood that a person was unable to swim, why would it bother to help a drowning human being?

One explanation that scientists have put forward for this kind of behavior is that dolphins are naturally curious and playful creatures. They often play with other dolphins.

A dolphin's flippers, which have bones similar to those of a hand, are mostly used for balance. Instead of pushing with their flippers, dolphins often play by pushing objects around with their pointy beaks. They often nudge each other while swimming. If a dolphin came across a drowning person, it might push the person ashore.

So, is the dolphin that saves a human life just playing? Or, does the dolphin realize it is helping a person in trouble? No one really knows for sure.

Another possible explanation for why dolphins sometimes come to the aid of drowning humans can be found in the way dolphins care for their newborns. Like all mammals, baby dolphins are born live—unlike most fish, which hatch from eggs laid in the water. When the baby is born, its mother or another dolphin may nudge it to the surface so it can take its first breaths. Perhaps this is how dolphins recognize that humans cannot breathe underwater.

Scientists do know that dolphins are very intelligent. Dolphins can figure out how to use tools they can hold in their beaks. For instance, they may use sharp fish bones as clippers to detach a bit of food off a rock. Scientists also know that dolphins are able to communicate with each other using a wide variety of sounds, including clicks, squeaks, and barks. Thirdly, scientists know that dolphins use echolocation underwater in much the same way that bats do in the air. To do this, a dolphin makes a series of high-pitched clicking sounds. These sounds bounce off its prospective dinner and return back to the dolphin. In its brain, these echoes form a picture. This picture allows the dolphin to distinguish what kind of fish is out there.

Dolphins are so intelligent that they can be trained to understand human commands. Memorizing very complicated instructions is not hard for them, just like it doesn't seem to be hard for dogs. Their trainers use rewards of fish to teach them complicated routines. They jump through hoops and stand in the water. Dolphins have been taught to perform for audiences, but they have also been trained to help people in other ways.

In South Africa, a professor trained two dolphins named Dimple and Haig to protect swimmers from sharks. If a group of wild dolphins is threatened by a shark, they will often act together to attack the shark. Dimple and Haig were trained not to attack the sharks but to act like sirens. They would warn people when they sensed a shark was close enough to be a threat.

Dimple and Haig received special training to perform their task. However, in some instances, dolphins have figured out ways to help people on their own.

Dolphins have been known to assist people who fish off the coast of Africa. There is a tasty fish about one pound in weight called a mullet. This fish swims near the shore in shallow water. Dolphins have been known to surround schools of the fish and herd them toward the waiting nets. Of course, the dolphins take their fair share of mullets, too.

Hundreds of years ago in Australia's Port Phillip Bay, on the country's southeastern coast, members of a group of Aboriginal, or native, Australians also fished cooperatively with dolphins. Today, the tribe no longer fishes there, but the dolphins of the bay still can be seen tossing fish onto the same shore.

Like people, dolphins are social animals. Their instinct is to form strong relationships with their families and other members of their pods.

Dolphins in the same pod play together, gather food together, and protect one another from enemies, such as sharks and orcas. Orcas are actually another species of dolphin, commonly referred to as killer whales. If dolphins are attacked, they will batter a shark with their bodies to injure or kill it.

Raising their young is another task in which dolphins cooperate. One female will watch over several other females' young while the adults leave to hunt.

In some rare cases, however, adult dolphins will leave their pods, choosing to spend much of their time by themselves or in the company of humans. These dolphins are known as solitary dolphins.

One of the first known solitary dolphins was Pelorus Jack, who lived off the coast of New Zealand in the late 19th century. Jack swam over to meet ships and steamers as they entered the Pelorus Sound harbor. Perhaps Jack was first attracted by the sound of their whistles. Jack would travel with the ships to a certain point in the ocean, about six miles out, and then turn around, never going any farther.

For almost 20 years, Jack entertained passengers on the passing ships by leaping and diving alongside the bow. Jack was never seen swimming with other dolphins. It seems that he only swam with the ships that sailed in Pelorus Sound.

Another solitary dolphin lived around the Florida Keys and swam through the canals that connected people's homes to the ocean. She was frequently seen around a particular dock, whose owners paid her a lot of attention. When she became a "friend" of the family, they began calling her Dolly.

Even though Dolly was a solitary dolphin, she was still playful. At the same time, she was very gentle and patient with the children. She even let the girls hold on to her fin as she pulled them around the canals.

Dolly also learned to catch rubber rings, fetch balls, and retrieve coins from the water. These are similar to the tricks dolphins are taught at amusement parks or aquariums.

Almost like a pet, Dolly seemed to understand when she was being scolded for being bad or being praised for doing something good. The family believed that Dolly understood simple words, such as "yes" and "no."

Because dolphins are so intelligent and easy to train, they have sometimes been given more serious tasks by humans, as well. The United States Navy eventually became interested in what dolphins could do. They began a training program involving dolphins in 1960.

The first "mission" by a Navy dolphin took place in 1965. A bottlenose named Tuffy carried tools to workers at the Navy's Sea Lab II, off the coast of La Jolla, California. In fact, he made the 200-foot dive repeatedly. Tuffy was also trained to guide lost divers to safety.

Other bottlenose dolphins have actually been trained to find mines that would blow up a large ship. When these dolphins detect a mine, they attach a line to it that is also attached to a floating buoy nearby.

Another task the Navy gave dolphins was to protect its ships. What could a nine-foot dolphin do for a steel aircraft carrier the length of a football field? It can guard the ship from underwater attack. When ships are in port, enemy divers sometimes attempt to attach explosives to them at night. These divers had often escaped detection. With their keen hearing, dolphins have been successful at locating such enemy divers easily.

During the Vietnam War, five Navy dolphins were brought to Cam Ranh Bay to patrol for divers in the water. Six dolphins went to the Persian Gulf in 1986 to patrol Bahrain Harbor. They also served as escorts for oil tankers.

These missions were considered secret. When American citizens found out about them, some criticized the Navy. These people claimed that it was cruel to use dolphins for military purposes because dolphins were being harmed during the training and on their missions. In the 1990s, the Navy decided it did not need as many dolphins.

Returning them to the wild, however, was not easy. Some dolphins had spent so much time with humans that they did not know how to feed themselves or how to act with wild dolphins. There was also the fear that they might infect other dolphins with a germ they got in their unnatural situations. Therefore, some of the dolphins were not released. They will live out the rest of their lives in the Navy's care.

Clearly, there are many ways in which dolphins help humans. We can train them to understand us by rewarding them with food if they do what we want them to do. Can they learn from us—can they understand *why* we want them to do something? Might we also learn from them?

Scientists still have no proof that humans and dolphins can actually talk to one another. Nevertheless, scientists continue to experiment with different methods of communication. One example is the hydrophone. This device can record and play back the dolphin's varied whistles and clicking noises. Other methods involve using hand signals and whistling sounds.

One thing is for certain, though. Dolphins know a great deal about the sea. If scientists ever managed to communicate with dolphins, we would be able to learn much about marine biology. Naturally, we hope that dolphins will also learn something in the bargain.